Love in the Age of Virtual Memory

Love in the Age of Virtual Memory

Poems by

Laura D. Weeks

Cover design by Shay Culligan
Cover image by Chris Weeks
Author photo by Sophia Weeks

ISBN: 978-1-63980-837-3
Library of Congress Control Number: 2025951499

Kelsay Books
502 South 1040 East, A-119
American Fork, Utah 84003
Kelsaybooks.com

for Carolyn Moore—
poet, mentor, friend

Acknowledgments

Every book is a product of many hands. Thanks to all those who gave a helping hand at various stages: April Ostmann, for bringing order out of chaos, Terry Lucas, for his insightful comments, Tom Daley, in whose workshops many of these poems were written, and the many friends, fellow poets and writing group members who contributed advice: Mary Christine Delay, Penelope Scambly Schott, Donna Prinzmetal, Dianne Stepp, Margaret Chula, Karen Braucher Tobin. Special thanks to my beloved family: Chris, Sophia, and the man of many names (IT Papa, Mr. Fix-it, the man who makes things work)–John Weeks.

With thanks to the readers and editors of the following journals in which these poems appeared in slightly altered form, or under different titles.

All We Can Hold (Sage Hill Press, 2016): "After the Slaughter"

Atlanta Review: "What Bones Want" (Finalist for the Rash Award)

Branches Quarterly: "The Mad Woman," "The Secret Life of Oranges"

The Chaffin Journal: "Self Portrait With Skulls"

Claudius Speaks: "What the Birds Sang to the Dead Girl Who Fell from a Tree"

Cloudbank: "Lopsided Tango"

Color Wheel: "House of Sound and Fog"

The Comstock Review: "Love in the Age of Virtual Memory"

The Journal of Kentucky Studies: "On the Origins of Speech," "Earthbound"

The MacGuffin: "What's the Russian for Horseradish?"

Mudfish: "Tsvetaeva's Chamber Pot"

Muse: "When Shadows Walk" (Honorable Mention for the Holden Vaugn Spangler Award)

the new renaissance: "That Room of One's Own"

Nimrod: "As I Thwack the Keys, I Sing," "Beethoven's Ghosts"

Port Yonder Press: "A Hand by Any Other Name" won honorable mention in the Zero Bone Poetry Prize.

The Worcester Review: "Sowbug"

Yes Poetry! (in an anthology honoring the seventh anniversary of the Silverton Poetry Festival, 2007): "Boltzmon's Last Set"

Contents

III

IV

I

Tomorrow's Forecast

A cold spleen moves over the deeps
trailing a scarf of fog
across the salt flats of my mind.
Pressure, as of a brooding storm,
batters my eardrums.
Sure as you might say,
"Looks like rain,"
or, "Feels like thunder!"
tomorrow I will writhe,
booming surf inside, vertigo
dogging uncertain steps.

Outside my head—
uncommonly quiet.
I can no longer tell
one sound from another:
barking dog? Bleating brass?
A handsaw's hollow rasp?—It's all one.
What sound comes,
threading an ever-smaller needle,
scars my hearing—a thin red streak of sound.
Tomorrow, I'll flounder in the swell;
tonight I ride

the eye of the storm.

“That Room of One’s Own”

Two large windows hung
with lemon-yellow curtains.
Yellow windows, yellow walls.
Saffron sprigged with innocence.

Yes, even the bookshelves.
My husband, laughing,
beard flecked with spackle:
“Guess there’s no need
to ask what color I should buy.”

Early morning—the best time.
Sun slipped round the corner
like a lady on her way out,
nodded to the room in passing.

Four years I kept that room alive,
heart tack-tacking on the keyboard.
Four years my blood dissolved in words.
Vitals flattened, yellow faded.

Sour aftertaste of lemon.

There Is No Marker Here

There is no marker here,
this rough trough, trenched
where shoulder slopes,
then rises to meet the road.

Ivy spills—a casket spray
over the mound.
Cold oaks work their arthritic joints,
scrape, scrape, scrape their scabby knees.

Woodsmoke censes the pearlescent sky
now as then. Above soft duff and detritus
a pyracantha branch
startles—a screaming scar.

Sound came later:
screech of witness, small moan,
the daughter stirring
beneath her mother’s protective bulk,

two whey-faced officers
sifting the aftermath.
Now as then
a car skims the shoulder,

close-shaves two figures walking there
then streams on,
leaving limp pink flesh
like an airbag deployed.

Beethoven's Ghosts

> *My bad hearing haunted me everywhere like a ghost*
> *and I fled—from mankind.*
> —a letter to Wegeler, November, 1801

Even at midnight
it's breakfast in my ear.
Sausage sizzles in the tympanum
releasing legions
of unnatural noises.
A gnat's thin, high-pitched whine
compounds the melee.
Whole and quarter tones war
with shades of now-stilled voices.

Everywhere they bedevil me!
Afternoons along the *Landstrasse*
in every promenading *mädchen* I see
her dear dead face—
my sister—childishly soft
brown hair, blue eyes
deep as heliotrope;
in every pram, my other self—
my infant brother
dead, and buried with my name.*

Evenings, in salons
or in the concert hall,
they gather, grouping
and regrouping, laughing
as they shoot provoking looks

my way. Some raise a glass to me,
one proffers a child's slate
as if to summon me
by automatic writing.

Once, when my hands wandered
lost among the forest
of white birch keys,
a hand no bigger than a toddler's
reached out and touched me
from behind.
So terrible, so slight
that touch, and clinging like warm wax.
I must have jumped a foot
before I ran.

No, I have it all backwards!
They, *they* are the living, while I—
I am a freak, a phantom in a frock coat,
born of a howl and a whimper,
and of my Father's ineluctable lust
for pure sound.
Never to be exorcised, I am
this stubborn ringing
in the celestial ear.

Basic Botany: Seven Names for a Chinese Lantern

They lay where they had fallen:
October's discards, hidden in dust
and detritus, except for their bright hearts.
Winter cherries!
Fit fruit for a grim November day.

Once a stem of Chinese Lanterns,
their brilliant calyxes now stripped
to skeletons by worms and weather:
a shell of delicate macramé, or netting,
or a lobster pot, the lobster fast inside.

I fingered one, and thought,
"Order solonales,"—sol,
sun suspended in a hollow globe,
like one we used
when taught to chart the stars.

I gathered three together,
turned their heads stem downwards.
They rose up,
three Russian onion domes,
their carmine tongues clacking the tocsin.

Japanese offer the lantern's seeds
as guides for the deceased,

to lead their souls, to where?
Seeds lead to birds, and right side up again
I saw a Scarlet Macaw in his cage.

Cage, yes, *that's* the needed image.
Not fretwork but rib cage, with heart
still squawking its deathless drivel.
The lantern's common name:
"Love in a Cage."

I thrust it into compost
just to silence it.

Madness Arrives via Express Mail

Thus they do not wait for letters,
Thus, they wait for A Letter.
—Marina Tsvetaeva

Somehow I knew this summons was for me.
The day dawned hot. Birds were out in force.
A warm wind trolled among the pines,
lifted their skirts, ran fingers up their legs.
The treetops laughed in ecstasy.

Then your letter came.

Midsummer madness fevered every page.
On every page, your voice—
low, like bumblebees humming Carmina Burana
while kissing the newly nippled hawthorn.

Stop this nonsense. Do not write again.
Or, if you do—

No. Against this day's slow, sweet intoxication

I am immune. See, I have promises to break,
and I am wedded to untroubled sleep.

Polystylistics in Five Easy Lessons

To the memory of Nina Iskrenko

Polystylistics is when we go to cross
a street in Moscow
& all the billboards are in English,
& some kid in his Polo shirt and jeans
yells, "Go home, Yankee!"
& all the billboards
stand up on their hind legs and bark
while all the cars stop in the intersection
& look on.

Polystylistics is when you ditch
the wife and kids
(just because you love them so much
you know what I mean?)
& I call the Doctor about my depression
& he says,
"Take two lovers, go to bed
& call me in the morning."

Polystylistics is when
I take the laundry
out of the dryer
& shake it out, all nice and smooth
& fold it neatly
down the garbage grinder.

Polystylistics is when
the universe turns inside out
like some enormous pillowcase
& you can see it’s
all sprinkled with God’s ~~dandruff~~
I mean stars
& hanging by a thread.

Polystylistics is when
a beautiful woman dies
& becomes a Sacred Text
good between the covers.

When Shadows Walk

Read only children's books.
Cherish only childish thoughts.
—Osip Mandelstam

Children fold up so small at night.
Their unquiet limbs,
stilled in impossible poses,
shrink from your touch like sea anemones.
The largest of them
could fit into your palm.

Their things, so underfoot
by day, at night acquire
a sudden gravity.
Dolls, becalmed, stare
with transatlantic eyes—
foreign emissaries conspiring quietly
in nooks, on bookshelves.

Children are adepts,
bypassing the possible
for the implausible.
Children are obsessive:
rules and rituals,
whiter whites,
deeper cuts.

When shadows patrol the halls
grown-ups see corridors,
closet doors, cellars, storage
steerage. Children see
wardrobes with *fur* trees,
attics, shipwrecks,
faces like fishes—
portholes for eyes.

The Mad Woman

There are souls not firmly in their bodies,
eyes vacant as an empty parking lot,
minds blasted by their own
immortality . . .

Deaf to every other sound, she stands
frozen at the dishpan, staring,
breasts and waist soaked with the soapy mess,
hearing only . . .

the sing-song of old man chaos—
holding fingers cut on coffee cans,
admiring the rainbow-colored blood.

No longer maid, no longer fair she stands,
with the world soul running out
like a broken egg between her feet.

After the Slaughter

Newtown, Connecticut, December 14, 2012

A mother is a plate
licked clean by many mouths.
A mother is comfort, clothed
in a hundred yards of madness.

She devotes her days
to mundane tasks
like sticking contacts in a tiger's eye,
or trading punches
with Old Man Chaos.

A mother counts:
infants' piggies, missing buttons,
supper servings, "times I've told you,"
the hours—from one to five.

From school's out till lights out she sits,
her mind a shallow bowl.
She considers
the sudden resonance of empty rooms.

She fingers flatware,
calling this fork "Frederick,"
and this spoon "Ernestine,"
while laying them lovingly
to rest in coffin slots.

A mother is a sock turned inside-out,
hung out to dry.
Listless, she scours sheets, searches
for her lost child's scent.

Love in the Age of Virtual Memory

What you have forgotten
never stays there long.
Memory scrabbles in its pockets,
turns the same loose coin
over and over . . .
Over neurons' wireless network
a signal rattles the cell phone
sleeping in its bone case.

Your voice, which has not aged,
falls instantly into the old banter:
fishing for more,
settling for less.

Meeting in the flesh: a thumbnail sketch,
a flicker of texting, eye to eye.
Our coverage has expanded
like our girth—colleagues,
kids, careers, your wife, my husband.
Our talk flows easily along shared bandwidths.

A crumpled coffee cup confirms the time.
With everything we lost,
or rather, because of it,
grace leavens our leave-taking.

A flaw in scripting snags my exit:
memory streaming in real time.
Small hands search your face,
trace the scar across your cheek.
Your half-strangled whisper,
"What will we call this?" "Sunstroke,"
my unheard reply.

II

The Secret Life of Oranges

Italian immigrant, day laborer—
round peasant face
varnished by sun and wind,
a single sunspot
on your pockmarked cheek.
By day, out of place
like a mislaid piece of backdrop.

By night you slip your skin,
ripping the Velcro to become
a French aristocrat
smooth as suede,
lavish with perfume.

Spremuta d'arancia, you were born
to make men's minds wander,
mouths go astray . . .
Let them eat their hearts out.
No one would guess
your heart holds huge chambers
full of fragrant tears.

Chairs

It is deep evening now.
In the shuttered dining room,
ranged against the wall,
mosquito hawks perched on thin legs,
they sit in after-dinner half-light,
lost in thought.

Their dance is done—
the daily thump and squee,
stick, then slide,
forward, up to the table,
embrace your partner,
and back.

Some unseen constraint
forbids them
to straddle the intervening distance,
change positions,
(much less partners),
circle left or right.

We are those chairs, dear,
kept in separate corners,
deaf to the dance.
When we were human
we shared the same chair.
Once.

As I Thwack the Keys, I Sing

She is as fragile as faience
sitting on my piano bench,
hair—red as Basho's lantern,
skin like fine rice paper.

A perfect miniature in porcelain
down to the deft calligraphy
around her crinkled eyes and nose
when she smiles.

Then, an encounter with her eyes.
Something shatters.
Behind thick chunks of glass they stare
like headlights—high beams straying
into oncoming traffic.

Frantic to undo the damage,
casting wildly about for a stone
to unlock her private language, I
surround her with my voice.

"No. Again. Remember, for a pianist
the ring finger is number four, not three."
She uncoils a moist fist, stretches
fingers that betray her.

"Here. Try this." I place
my long loose-jointed bamboo shoots
over her slim white tubers,
manipulate both hands together.

As I thwack the keys, I sing.
She stares, all eyes, into my mouth,
rounds her small plum blossom into a howl.
Music issues from her blasted mind.

Why Reading the News Is Like Watching an Opera

F is laughter—
pure lavish pleasure,
a splash of adrenaline,
a flash of mermaid's coda.
Or, exuberant host—equally at home
tickling a salmon or poaching a hare.

G is gracious—
a grin grafted onto sorrow's face,
a great grief lifted,
a grain of forgiveness in this savage place.
Mercy—like a green grace note
in a sour world.

A is playful—
a bracing bourrée, a game of tag played
allegro con brio. A blithe repartee,
a slice of vivacious
conversation. Escapades
of a lady gone astray.

B fie foe fum,
here I come, stumblebum.
Some dumb cherub,
unable to plumb
love's excesses
or its wisdom.

C Sharp is cruelty—
Queen of Spades, spitting invective,
skilled at curses and quarrels,
spills her crucible
full of slender insinuations—
scalds her own kids.

D Sharp is drama—
masquerade ending in a dozen deaths;
grenades lobbed by destiny's forces.
Buzz-cut boys offer themselves
in a fit of rustic chivalry,
to slaughter orchestrated behind the scenes.

Silence is white.
Isis of a thousand names
slides on her shining skin,
slips down a silken ladder:
descent into Tethys' realm
where pearl fishers flutter opalescent limbs.

A Letter from the Far Side of the Sofa

The clear blue envelope
of your eyes
lands in my lap.
Sky-blue tri-fold marked
not *"par avion"* but "URGENT."
Startled, I look up,
flinch before reading.

Time was,
such dispatches were simple,
franked communication:
"I'm tired." "Hold me."
These days, they're more likely
unexploded ordnance.

From my outpost, I send
a tentative, old-fashioned telegram.
Letters in formation cut
thin swaths across the plain
brown paper:
"Can't you just trust me?"

I cannot trust myself to see
my courier safely over the palisade:
your slim scrunched-up
limbs, sharp knees and elbows.
Another blue envelope.
The time for parley is past.

Self Portrait with Skulls

Kali has four arms,
but I have five tongues,
and I can curse in any one of them.
Careful! I might fix you
with my round eyes
full of malice.

I have a childlike psyche
changeable and clear
like aspic on a plate,
an unassuming nature—
puts people off their guard.

I am at my ruthless best
in academic hothouses
where false tropes
bloom among the marginalia.
If some slim lie slinks into the room—
Kali bursts from Durga's forehead
wielding her steel-armored tongue.

I might as well be
foaming at the mouth,
speaking in tongues.
Still, I sit, fingering my beads,
my exotic rosary of skulls,
each one a severed department head.

Sometimes I am overcome
by an urge
to peel the covers off creation,
kick the continents awake,
unscrew the planets from their sockets,
set them adrift . . .

I long to clap, to stomp, to howl,
to dissolve in dance.
Then I am in my element:
Mad Mistress of a world
out of control.

On My Fourth Rejection in as Many Days

Primitive bards had it easy:
skinned language like a fox,
doffed the fur, made music on the bones.

In another age they rode,
whooping like warriors
among stars clacking like castanets.

Fists gripped the comet's gritty tail,
while the comet hummed comfortably
in its meteor shower.

Fast forward—bards became shooting stars,
each boy falling on his blade
of grass, for some dim myth
called England . . .

Those doors are locked
that held *that* kind of magic.
Which leaves me

fumbling with keys,
mistress of a thousand and one rewrites . . .
That's it. Scheherazade.
How would she begin?

At my back door, words
like cats
wait to be let in.

Ode to the Common Tater

After Neruda

O, you thrice-blessed apple of the earth,
child of the Andes
cradling your hidden star,
how far you have fallen.

High-born, yet banished
to servants' quarters, your smock's
rough homespun yields
to your master's eager hands, reveals
flesh coarse as unbleached linen.

Colonizer of continents!
Stowed in ships' holds you sailed
from the New World to the Old
and back again.

There they saddled your round shoulders
with the humble appellation "Spud,"
like the all-too-common "Bud." Or "Bub," "Bubba . . ."
Bubbling in frothy kitchen oceans,
you bless the masses,
bring kings and commoners to their knees

in praise of earth.
For the grave is her mouth, but you—
you are her eyes.
Strange eyes that see strange transformations:

flesh flakes from bones
like sheets of mica,
grubs, diggers, maggots,
larvae blossom,
winging into thought.

Noble *kartoffel,* storehouse of earth's goods,
you are mother to that apple
full of all wisdom, full of all peril.
As above, so below.

Live Fat. Die Thin.
(Callas Does an Encore at the Trattoria)

"Take this plate of slops!
Feed it to the poor, to the rats,
I don't care! Tonight I crave
an orgy of pasta lusty with sauce,
just to appease my palate,
that great Gothic arch.
You do know who I am?!"

Still the diva, even though
they all jumped ship:
the voice, the lovers, the svelte
curves, but this remains.
True, I was voracious: I devoured
every rival's ego whole,
a snake swallowing an egg.

I must have got that from my mother,
"saintly" Evangelia, who starved me
four days at birth, then fed me on her venom.
At five she had me singing for my supper.
At fifteen she pimped me out to soldiers,
while she pocketed my gleanings:
a chocolate bar, a pack of cigarettes . . .

Back then, I was a big, slow-moving barge.
My huge nose plied my face—
a rowboat, oars lofting out over my eyes.
Even my voice was thick—
A sweet dark river of molasses.
And I was always hungry.

Then I recast myself as "La Divina,"
shucked the pounds, pared down the voice;
ah, what fearsome beauty.
How I could spin the *canto spianato*:
hold the high E in *Vespri*
until it faded at the edges,
like an ink blot on white paper.

Maybe it was the tapeworm
eating at my entrails. All I know,
my life, once unrivaled, unraveled
like cheap silk. The edges of my voice
frayed to a snarl, a whine, a shriek,
my chest caved in—a vacant concert hall . . .
And still the beast needs feeding.

A Hand by Any Other Name

with apologies for riffing off (ripping off) Tsvetaeva

A hand is a mandate
for communication:
the original iPhone,
where your cells meet mine.

It's a textbook, a manual,
a "how-to" for lovers
only slightly less potent
than a little black look.

A hand is a contract:
seal the deal with the right,
steal the till with the left.
Just be sure you're not left

stranded. Abandoned.
Hands that master
the strictures of writing
unlearn how to love.

Take the plunge. Slip your skin.
Enter love like one hand
gently enters another's.
Leave the back door ajar:

Baby, I'd love to,
but my hands are tried
and true. I'm a secondhand Juliet
with her palmed-off pun

destined for some *manus* crypt.

Beethoven at the Pianoforte

The year 1805. After a performance of Pleyel's latest quartets, Beethoven is dragged to the pianoforte by the ladies and asked to improvise. His listeners are overwhelmed, including old Pleyel, who wordlessly kisses Beethoven's hand. Czerny writes, "His attitude at the pianoforte was perfectly quiet and dignified, with no approach to grimace, except to bend down a little towards the keys as his deafness increased. In rapidity of scale passages, trills, leaps, no one equaled him . . . after such improvisations Beethoven was wont to break out in a loud and satisfied laugh."

Feet well-planted,
fingers splayed,
I rise out of myself
like some great flowering tree,
taproot sunk deep
below the floorboards,
crown inclined,
while fresh leaves flutter
over the keyboard.
Flutter deepens into double trills,
unfolds in runs and ripples.
The air shivers in ecstasy.

Now the sap rises
like beer—a healthy head of foam!—
thunders in my ears,
flushes in face and fingertips.

I am intoxicated,
root and bole, branch and bough.
This—no earthly brew—
libation worthy of the gods!
Come, Muses, who will be the first
to give herself to me?
Let straining guy wires snap!
Mediocrities, back off!

It is over.
I am released.
My laughter scatters light as leaf fall
on their bewildered faces.
But the burdened air
holds the final pitch
still throbbing
in its fist.

III

Insomnia

Insomnia. Homer. Taut sails.
I've read the list of ships halfway through . . .
—Osip Mandelstam

That was the summer I finally learned
sleeping is an art
like swimming, sailing, rollerblading.

It takes a great gift
to black-out intellect
while words flux out of the air,
their shrill flutter
scattering like seagulls
over the estuary of pure thought.

Speech lies dormant.
The bay spreads out—
a pregnant woman's rounded knee
crisscrossed with spider veins,
full of the salt water of compliance—
timeless marriage of mind and sand.

The water rises,
drowning hordes
of incandescent syllables.
Waves of strange sonorities sweep in
over the reef.

On the Origins of Speech

Soil is all language—
damp, intractable,
until the developer comes
slashing the tense, fibrous sod,
sowing verbs—
pale livid bulbs
with threads of thought still hanging.

They thrust upward,
their vulgar little noses
pushing, probing,
splitting the skin
to reveal
mouths wide open in surprise.

But the grass is master of semantics,
and of the pregnant pause.
Delaying its grand entrance,
it sends out little tongues,
moist, pointed,
to interrogate the weather.

Grass is all eloquence—
pure sweet-talk,
even as we bruise it.

Tsvetaeva's Chamber Pot

Maybe, the best victory
Over time and gravity
Is just to slip by, and leave no trace.
—Marina Tsvetaeva

To let: one room. Three flights up. No bath.
A squalid quarter of Clamart.
And there, dead center of the room,
round and redolent, and brimful,
a chamber pot.

An oversight? Maybe you hoped
as you hunkered down at night
after a meal of horses' testicles,
given the general stench of Parisian slums,
it would go overlooked?

Strange. You who preached
the clean getaway—"slip by and leave no trace"—
left this most life-affirming dung.
You, who ordered verbs around like serving girls—
balked by the verb "to be."

A tribute to things physical? Or a rebuke
from the body you so lightly wore—
a paper doll's dress suspended by thin tabs—
and just as lightly shed.

Writing Dad's Obit

How could you walk out on me?
When they wheeled you in—
rubber soles stalking the sterile silence—
you hadn't a leg to stand on.

Just last week you drove
your walker like a plow,
torso all tense determination,
feet curling fretfully, hefting their fetters.

Is this one of your out-of-body stunts?
Christ knows you read enough
to write the book on that,
leaving me as footnote.

What's with this most pedestrian of poses?
"Consummate mathematician conned
by plain geometry"—the jaw's oblique angle,
eyes' pale sunken octagons—
cheesecloth stretched over a chickenwire frame.

Only your forehead rests,
swathed in moths' wings of purest white . . .
an old man's hair . . .
your lips still primed to speak.

This conversation is *so* not over.
Give me a hand. Here. I'll haul you upright.
Take these two solid columns.
Walk out on them.

Twisted Tales from the Vienna Woods: Rieu's Orchestra plays the Emperor's and Skaters' Waltzes

A tableau of purest German marzipan:
curved rows of creamy women in crinoline
flanked by men in full armor.
Double rows of glossy heads,
white shirt fronts . . . eggs in a carton!

First stirrings, first stuttering rhythms.
Deft as a dentist, the flautist
taps his golden crowns.
The conductor turned doctor
feels for, finally finds
his fiddle's pulse.

And we're off, with a bit of swagger, a martial strut!
Then—*molto rubato*—
a theme sweet as snowfall
melts in the arms
of a sweltering cellist,
swooning in spotlight.

After the Kaiser, we switch to the *Schlittshue,*
the "fleet shoes," and the *Schlittenfahrt.*
The fiddles skitter around
like farts in a skillet
accompanied by bad ass antics in the brass.

The percussion surrender
to barnyard chaos. Cartoon-thin lamb's legs
scamper over the timpani,
while the snare drummer shakes the cluckin' spiel,
and cymbals blow kisses to the crowd.

Now ideal becomes idyll.
The Viennese vision of blond elegance
reveals its rural roots:
not the Kaiser's slick ballroom,
but the fairgrounds, the kermess.

It's all country matters:
rump-a-thump washboard rhythms,
brown bread and brown ale,
drunken villagers
doing the barrel turn.

Small wonder Beethoven
tearing his hair out cried,
"Just give them their little brown sausages!"
Even then, Vienna
was not what it used to be.

Sowbug

But as for you most odious—
Would Blake call you holy?
—Theodore Roethke

The failing light feeds lines,
stage whispering
to the leaves, who promptly start
speaking in tongues.

Out of dank recesses
in the rock wall
you make your entrance,
like a bad actor, fumbling along.

Sowbug! Your very shape
revolts me! A sausage cased
in armor—soft, corrupt.
All cilia and belly.

Admit it, you love
dishing the dirt, chewing decay,
churning out pulp
like some hack writer.

Tickled, you pill,
curl around the vulnerable
center of your obscene
existence.

Sowbug! Your performance
prompts my deepest fear:
all art is Jonah
calling from the belly.

What the Birds Sang to the Dead Girl Who Fell from a Tree

Let go of gravity.
Feel it shudder down your limbs,
pool at your ankles,
now you are ours.
Henceforth, you too will dream
only of singing.

Here you will find
new modes of being
between flesh and fletch,
between the invisible and the unfeasible—
here in Dreamtime,
what we call home.

There are no laws here,
except those of flight;
no weight except
the burden of song.
Or, as we teach fledglings:
first the cadenza,
then the reprise.

Begin by imitating:
tweak the predictable pattern
with subtle violations.
Transcribe the language of birdsong by day;
read it out at night.
Debate the virtue of sleep in humans,
of dream vs. flight.

Sound Waves

As I lay on the surgeon's gurney,
my flesh and I for once at peace,
I heard it. In the crow's nest of my ear

I heard it: regular, unhurried,
rhythmic as the suck and pull of tide.
"Squee-squee," then soft and quick, "thup-thup."
My mother and her dry mop swab the floors.

And I am eight. Sick. Bedridden.
Woozy head and oozing ears.
The slightest movement on my part—
riptides carve a scar across the swash.

This is how she likes me. Not the pain,
but my unnatural compliance.
My unquiet limbs stilled, for once,
while she stills her unquiet mind.

This is our bargain, our unspoken pact:
I allow her minimal control;
she corrals the sweepings of her past.

When I am not as sick, I pretend.
I admire tidal pools of light,
dust motes light as spindrift in her wake.

It’s fifty years since. My now crippled ears
hobble over barren sands
washed by waves of vertigo,
stung by high-pitched siren’s song.

Time’s up. It’s time to go. Unwilling wheels
screech to attention. Even before
the sneaker wave betrays me,
I know what I will hear. I hear it still.

I hear.

Lopsided Tango

What shall I do with my one lone pinion?
Trust me, it isn't easy
to hide up your sleeve,
though I have been known
to toss it casually across my body
in homage to Erte's glossy gowns.

It's not much good
for signing checks or clearing tables,
and it can be downright awkward:
how to manage a handbag, for instance,
or, worse yet, a handshake.

What is the point of its existence?
It should be the stuff of legend,
subject of fairy-tales, instead—
it's more of a shrieking tabloid headline:
"Athena springs, half-armed
From Zeus' head!"

These days I’m finding it unreliable.
I’ve grown deaf to its demands,
following me around like a whining teenager
or drooping like a dispirited dust rag.
But lately I swear
it wants to smother me in my sleep.

So, to keep the peace,
on warm somnolent evenings,
or when a cold moon calls
the partridge to take flight,
we dance. Now leading, now following,
it drags me round the floor,
writing my name in the dust.

What's the Russian for Horseradish?

"KHREN"—nose hairs bristle
at the salty sting of recognition.
Russians like it hair-raising hot.
By iron-clad custom,
after the gut rush you gasp,
"Whew! I see Moscow!"
And yes, it brings tears.

Me? I don't see Moscow exactly.
For me horseradish
travels in a crowd,
descending like a party
already in full swing.

Here's sweet rich rye
wrapping herself around every guy she meets.
Here's startling garlic
mincing everyone with his sharp remarks.
Here's dill, draping herself gracefully
over roots of every color;
mushrooms tarted up
in pickling brine.

Khren uncorks childhood
memory so stoppered,
it spurts from the bottle
like a curse
unheard in the general din.

I see the kitchen invade
the quieter confines of the living room:
scalding steam encounters
mellow tobacco smoke
pearling from my father's pipe.
Instantly they clinch,
writhe, tangle, twine,
locked in holy acrimony . . .

bringing tears of a different order.

Flanders Field, This Time with Sunflowers

Russian Separatists Down Flight MH17

The boys of the Donbass walk tough,
wear names like Ruslan,
or Serge. Buff, bare-chested,
They strut their stuff.

The boys of the Donbass wear big boots,
bear big grudges,
lie like troopers,
shoot borrowed BUKs.

The boys of the Donbass talk terse:
"Maintain perimeter. Understood?
Keep civilians out." "Yes, Sir!"
"A passenger plane?" In our air corridor?"

They pick through littered skin,
sift burned rags from burned bones,
shuffle backpacks, boarding passes,
while foreign names fall
from their mouths like shells
of sunflower seeds.

The boys of the Donbass scatter like flak,
make sure their Mother
covers their backs.
Old Mother Russia,

mouthful of myths,
seeds fields with death;
sends sunflowers
to feed on rotting flesh.

Beethoven on His Deathbed

My beloved friend! Rest content now, for the memory of the past has taken hold of me . . .
—a letter to Wegeler, December 1826

I

Where did all the music go?
There used to be so much . . .
You had only to turn
a discerning eye
to see the whole world
passing in review:

trees like tuning forks
in different pitches
humming down the sky;

eggs all lined up
in their carton—
choirboys in a row.

The merest canine could conduct,
twirl his baton, till all the beasts joined in
a symphony of noses, ears and tails.

And I—I was generalissimo,*
Grand Marshall of it all,
the one whom every sound obeyed,

whose presence guaranteed
all the players—plants and planets,
stones and constellations—knew the score.

The show would go on
as planned.

> *After Beethoven had lain unconscious, the death rattle in his throat . . .*
> *there came a flash of lightning accompanied by a violent clap of thunder,*
> *which garishly illuminated the death chamber.*
>
> —Anselm Huttenbrenner, in a letter to Thayer

II

"Whatever happened?
I hardly recognize myself
these days . . ." Cantankerous old fart
raging in gassy impotence, I address

the long twilight in my ears.
Confined to senseless regimens,
surrounded by stumble-bums—
doctors and their eternal

bad advice, I am deprived
of feeling—my tears
awash in a sea of bile;
my universe narrowed
to the space between meals,

Polyhymnia reduced
to a rumble in the guts
a restless fidget
of the feet and knees.

What now? Lightning?
But no sound . . . ? Come, kettle drums!
Timpani, lend me your thunder!
The general, summoned
to an audience,

craves your accompaniment.
Powers and principalities, here is my fist!
Did you seriously believe
I would come quietly?

IV

Hitting the Wall at the Boston Marathon
April 15, 2013

Do not be afraid . . . the blood has already seeped down into the earth.
And there where it spilled, clusters of grapes are already growing.
—Mikhail Bulgakov, *The Master and Margarita*

Not a sound from the pavement.
Streets spool out from Faneuil Hall,
each with its tourniquet
of yellow tape.
Not a single car or cruiser,
no circulation rumbles down the arteries.

Boston lies becalmed in harbor.
The statehouse grieves,
head sunk on its knuckled fist,
gold in the cold late-winter sun.

Underground, the city's vast sciatic nerve—
stilled. No tremor of approaching trains,
no sea of arms and legs swells
into welcoming doors.
No voice tolls the passing stations:
Haymarket. Government. Park Street. Boylston . . .

This is how it ends.
After-shock.
The city shudders,
shakes its phantom limbs.

Earthbound

Why this sudden lust?
Desire gone dormant, frozen
in its bed by overwintered limbs
half-primed to bite the dust—we sprout
an unexpected love of gardening.

Our house is built, bought up
by years of grubbing in the trenches
hoping to hit pay dirt.
Why this sudden itch to pull up stakes,
go searching for new digs?

Scattered our small stock
of wit—advice no longer needed.
Our once captive audience
flowered and flown, hence we hunger
to commune with a tomato.

Humid hands revel in discovery—
shard and stone, shell and bone,
a buried wedding ring . . .
Our fingers sift through immortalities
as through a catalog.

And still soil speaks to us
in some forgotten tongue
heard *in utero*—familiar, urgent,
more intimate than childhood
when we dug halfway to China.

We come away spent
yet satisfied,
with little more in hand than this:
Wings for the seedling. Fire for the fertile.
Loam for the old.

Coastal Ode

Midday in Friday Harbor.
Crisp linen napkins snap
like sails luffing in the wind.
Ice cubes yaw in water goblets—
buoys slipping their mooring.

Berthed on bluffs above,
we drink in the sights:
the honest stench of trawlers,
tour boats bright as bling
on any Oscar crowd
with paparazzi seagulls in their wake.

The ferry bellows its approach,
coughs up cars and passengers:
Mother Mouthbrooder
blurting out hatchlings
stashed in her mouth for safekeeping.

Another hoarse sigh—
the ferry nudges out again
among tall-masted rigs,
row on row of sun-white
crosses, close-clustered
like some vast maritime cemetery.

All this miracle of nautical bustle
blistered with salt and light
hums beneath a near invisible veil of gold.
While we drown our senses
in the wine dark swill.

Boltzmon's Last Set

It all happened way back,
back when Boltzmon
was frontman
for the Sisterhood of the Traveling Pants.

He'd slip out between sets
grab a cute little number in the crowd,
slide behind the counter
still be-boppin' a-chatterin'

—wired, I tell you!—
head still snappin',
fingers still walkin' the moons
between the changes.

Us? We chugged our beer, quiet-like,
but Boltzmon, he never touched nothin'.
(Never needed it, neither!)
"Not while I'm workin', boys."

Then he'd shimmy on up to the stage,
firecracker eyes, smile so wide
you could number the stars.
"You're a beautiful crowd!"

Christ, that boy could charm!
His words slid glissando
over their foreheads.
"You want more music?"

"Yea-ah-ah!" Then the drums start talkin':
kunga and bongo,
djembe and tom-tom
flim-flam-a diddle and didgeridoo

till your scalp flips open,
your brains take a hike,
but your feet stay planted
on account of the vibes,

those oh-so-low vibes
crawlin' up your leg.
Boltzmon, Boltzmon,
nobody seed the subtle knife comin'.
Nobody knowed
it was the summer to die.

Exclusive Interview with Beethoven's Hair

You want to know what it was like,
my Rip Van Winkel years,
or, you should pardon the expression,
my Snow White act,
asleep in my glass coffin?

When the old man died,
(Now *there* was a *mensch!*
How he fought! To the end!)
came a silence like you've never seen:
doctors, fiddlers, friends, even his servant,
ankle-deep in sodden straw, choking
on the sweet-and-sour sickroom stench. *Feh!*

Pianissimo, the boy crept up,
marveling at his own *chutzpah*
eyes fixed squarely on me,
scissors prisoned in his shaking hand.
He tugged. I gave in.

Next thing I knew—entombed in glass!
Black three-inch oval, paper backing,
inscribed, no less: *My father cut this hair*
from Beethoven's corpse the day after his death . . .
Oy, gevalt! To be trotted out from time to time
like some *verschluginer* rich uncle!

—Do I remember any one event?
Does any incident stand out?—
October, forty-three. A Danish fishing village.
Darkness fingering their flesh,
salt air prying into clothes and nostrils,
an overwhelming smell—
wet wool and fear—a purely human smell.

They huddled, calves already marked
for slaughter.
Then a slamming and a hammering,
the harsh imperatives of German jackboots,
the forked lightning of betrayal.

I myself escaped,
passed clandestinely
from palm to palm.
Cooled my heels some fifty years
in *Herr Doktor*'s desk drawer.

—And then what?— And then—celebrity!
Imagine: a star turn at Sotheby's,
among the curiosities and *tchotchkes*
the one, the only living relic—
I cleared three thousand pounds and some.

From auction to action: TV crews,
cameras, anchormen, journalists jostling,
gesturing—an Oscar worthy crowd
to film my grand opening,
everyone reverent, riveted
as the surgeon slit the sealed glass.
Out I popped
as fresh as the day I was shorn!

—I'd like to know—I'll bet you do!
What finally killed the great man?
I'm saving the best for last . . .
First, my radioimmunoassay,
my appointment with the x-ray spectrometer . . .

Forensic pathologists—they know from nothing.
They're used to dealing with such low-lifes,
such *schnorrers.*
While *I* . . . *I* am the ultimate scoop,
live coverage from beyond the grave!
I have such things to tell
like you wouldn't believe.

What Bones Want

For Mary Christine Delea

Air, primarily.
Tired of doing time
in the moist sweatshop of the flesh,
they pry open a window—
a fracture of an inch, no more—
poke an elbow
through skin's sleeve.

Then, they want out.
Miners trapped in the chest's cavern,
probe with picks,
feel their way through decades
to the surface.
One eye on the caged bird,
they gauge what time is left.

Bones crave certainty.
Unruly children, they invent
a world where explanations
are cut and dried, rules—hard and fast.
Acutely curious,
they crack open a door,
eavesdrop on the doctor's drone.

Their idea of a good time?
Kicking around the knacker yard,

complete with hot tub
where fluids boil away like lies,
where they emerge virtuous
and clean—a mere shimmer of pearl
fit for a reliquary.

A Short History of Lime

Lime, the smooth operator,
oozing coolness, cruises the room,
adds zest to the gossip, jazzes his guests
for their lost inhibitions.

Child of the tropics,
lime worn symbol of the South:
Key West, Key Largo, and Key Lime pie,
black boys in white suits woo their girls
under Savannah skies.

Lime—the indispensable
element in physic and cuisine:
little Brit in a pith helmet,
the *sine quinine* in the cure for malaria.

Hero of a legendary age,
who vanquished scurvy single handed,
now retired, potters about the kitchen.
Surprisingly tart, his acid wit
keeps fruit from fainting.

Lime, the world traveler,
voyager on every ship,
takes on the patina of mystery,
green of ocean,
sheen of tortoiseshell.

Shipwrecked mariner,

boat crushed by ice floes,
lies on the bottom—sunken treasure
bathed in softly filtered limelight,
his jade pale flesh
adrift in the drink.

So You Want to Write an Old Age Poem?

First, forget the kitsch—
the red hat and the purple.
The real thing clinks along
on gimpy knees and swollen feet.

Next, don't expect logic.
This poem bares its teeth.
Then, when you turn your back, it hides
in a box on your bedside table
next to the oxygen and the antacid.

Make no mistake, this poem's got moxie.
Firmly planted in the crosswalk,
it heckles oncoming traffic,
shaking a walking stick at SUVs.

Prone to serious lapses in syntax,
it falls asleep in the produce aisle,
jolts awake at sundowning.
Now is your chance
to get a leg up, provided you

watch your back. This poem will haunt you
like a leaking sink
until the plumber comes with tubes and needles
to snake your soul out your nose.

Finally, add something subtle, furtive:
an old woman licking the rim
of a jam jar, craving
the sweetness she once was.

Grandmother's Summer

Now the fruit hangs within reach.
Thin threads of cloud
crochet their way across the sky.
Sun settles on the edge of his chair—
a guest who overstayed his welcome—
babbles belated blessings on his hosts.

Now the housewife's fertile hands
hover fretfully
among her gathered gear:
rings, tongs, lids, vat,
spoon swirling the sweetness—the backs of plums
are turtles swimming in the wine-dark swill.

The year burns and shines,
but at a distance—
a Ferris wheel hijacked
at the height of its turning,
reveals the midway,
all flash and foil below.

Russians call it "Grandmother's Summer:"
an aged grande dame, throned in wicker, half-asleep
leans, loosens stays and corset,
offers her flesh to the warm wind
that softly lofts the crop
of finest golden hair lining her limbs.

House of Sound and Fog

Music is feeling, then, not sound.
Tell me you've never felt it:
crickets' descant
(airplanes humming *sotto voce* overhead),
raindrops deft as pointe shoes
patterning the Marley floor;
birdsong, windsong, ocean's toccata,
the soft nocturne of highways
spiraling to sleep.

But for the moment,
forget your bells and whistles.
The real thrill is here—
this jack-hammer racketing, girder clanging,
backhoe jangling, beeping, backing,
engine idling, siren whining,
heel-clacking, cell phone nattering
boom box, mind-boggling
street symphonics.

Face it, we live
in a house of sound,
where words are just false flooring;
where all activities sink into sound,
indispensable for reading
its vital signs:
infants' and lovers' *vocalise,*

a sick child's breathing,
an old man's threnody.

Sound is element, then, as much as air.
Real stillness is water.
Immerse yourself—
you'll come up gasping.

What is your favorite sound?
Does it have heft and color?
Can you play snare drums
on upturned plates with chopsticks
in a crowded sushi shop?
What will you say
when they tell you,
"This is the last sound
you will ever hear?"

Notes

p. 9 Beethoven had both a brother and a sister who died in infancy. The presence of the dead brother, christened Ludwig Maria, gave rise to some rather spectacular mental gymnastics on Beethoven's part, including his deliberate denial of his actual birth date.

p. 13 Polystylistics is the brainchild of the Russian Modernist poet Nina Iskrenko, one of the founders of Moscow Club Poetry and arguably one of the most influential poets in recent decades. In her own words, polystylistics involves "a multiplicity of viewpoints, all bogged down in mutual discord and contradiction, and none mandated to assume a leading role," "the intrusion of filthy prose into unsullied poetry," and finally, "mistakes that violate the harmonious serenity, or exposition or, at the very least, its structural predictably." Nina Iskrenko died in 1995, of breast cancer, at the age of forty-four.

p.43 Beethoven bestowed military titles on his musical colleagues which appear in his correspondence. The publisher Anton Steiner was "Lieutenant General." Composer-publisher Tobias Haslinger was "Adjutant." He himself was "Generalissimo."

p. 44 Beethoven's last living act was to raise his fist as if to defy—what? God? Death? The world he was leaving?

p. 46 The remarkable saga of a lock of Beethoven's hair is taken from Russell Martin, *Beethoven's Hair*. (London: Bloomsbury, 2000). The night referred to is what the Danes call "the night of waiting," a night during WWII, when they evacuated hundreds of Jews bound for the camps to safety in Sweden.

About the Author

Laura D. Weeks is a recovering academic who moved West and moved on. Originally a Slavist with a Ph.D. from Stanford University, she has turned her hand to a variety of diverse pursuits: translating, editing, and running a piano studio, Weeks' Wunderkinder.

Her translations (scholarly and literary) have appeared in *Russian Literature Triquarterly, The Literary Review, South Central Review,* and *the new renaissance.* She coedited and translated for the anthology *Crossing Centuries: The New Generation in Russian Poetry* (Talisman House Press, 2000). She coedited *The Great Uncluttering: The Collected Poetry of Carolyn Moore* (PCC Panther Press, 2022).

Her poetry has appeared in numerous journals, including the *Atlanta Review, Claudius Speaks, The Comstock Review, Journal of Kentucky Studies, Passager, Pegasus, The MacGuffin, Mudfish, Nimrod, the new renaissance,* and *the Worcester Review.* It has also been anthologized in *All We Can Hold* (Sage Hill Press, 2016). She has been a finalist/semi-finalist for the Rash Award, the Zero Bone Competition, and the *Muse* Poetry Competition. She is the author of two chapbooks, *Deaf Man Talking* and *The Mad Woman.*

www.ingramcontent.com/pod-product-compliance
Lightning Source LLC
LaVergne TN
LVHW051014080826
845145LV00009B/2621

* 9 7 8 1 6 3 9 8 0 8 3 7 3 *